The
Outdoor Secrets
Companion
A Living Science Handbook

by
Karen Smith and Sonya Shafer

The Outdoor Secrets Companion
© 2010, Karen Smith and Sonya Shafer

Cover Design: Ruth Shafer

ISBN 978-1-61634-098-8

Published and printed by
Simply Charlotte Mason, LLC
P.O. Box 892
Grayson, Georgia 30017-0892
United States

SimplyCharlotteMason.com

Introduction

During the elementary years, your science lessons should accomplish three things:
1. Nurture within the child a sense of wonder at God's creation.
2. Cultivate a habit of careful observation.
3. Lay the groundwork of personal experience that will support future science studies.

The lessons in this book strive to accomplish those three goals. They are intended for children in First and Second Grades and are based on the gentle and interesting living science stories found in *Outdoor Secrets*, a book originally published in 1903. We have simply collected some additional ideas to encourage you and your child to explore more about the plants and animals and weather that the stories introduce. We have also included some nature poetry to enrich your discoveries.

Feel free to progress through the lessons at your own pace. If your child devours anything scientific, you might do several lessons each week. If you want to enjoy a more leisurely pace, you might do one lesson per week. Or you might do two or three lessons during one week, then do only one the next week. Whatever you decide, you have freedom. Do what works best for your family.

And along those same lines, remember that you don't have to do every idea that is suggested in the lessons. They are just suggestions; you may pick and choose from them as you are interested and able.

At the time of this publishing, all the book suggestions listed in the lessons were in print (unless otherwise noted). If you perhaps cannot find one of the titles, feel free to substitute a different book on the same topic.

We hope you enjoy these additional ideas that will encourage your child to continue exploring outdoor secrets!

Check out our Web site for links to more information on the topics covered in this book:
simplycharlottemason.com/books/outdoor-secrets/links-tips

A Word about Nature Notebooks

Throughout the lessons in this book you will see a reference to a nature notebook. A nature notebook is simply a blank sketchbook to begin with. It will become the child's personal record of what he observed and made a personal relation with during these studies.

Here are some key points to remember about a nature notebook.
1. A nature notebook is the child's own possession. It is not to be graded or criticized. It is not the parent's project; it belongs to the child.
2. A nature notebook can contain written observations, drawings, poetry, Scripture, specimens—whatever interests the child and encourages him to look closely and carefully at nature.
3. If the child isn't able to or comfortable with writing his observations in his nature notebook, the parent can do the writing as the child dictates what he wants to say.

Resources Needed

For the entire study

- *Outdoor Secrets* by Margaret P. Boyle
- *Favorite Poems Old and New* selected by Helen Ferris—This wonderful collection of poems will be a handy resource for your entire homeschooling career. We have had ours for more than fifteen years and still use it. A great investment!
- Nature notebook, one for each person (See page 7 for details.)
- (optional) *The Handbook of Nature Study* by Anna Botsford Comstock—This resource, that is available free online, is more of a reference book for the teacher to study to learn about the plants or animals ahead of time. Some lesson ideas are also given. Corresponding pages are listed for your convenience if you would like to use this resource as a supplement.

For specific lessons (Check your library)

- *How Do Apples Grow* by Betsy Maestro
- *Johnny Appleseed* by Reeve Lindbergh
- *A Desert Scrapbook: Dawn to Dusk in the Sonoran Desert* by Virginia Wright-Frierson
- *An Earthworm's Life* by John Himmelman
- *A Seed Is Sleepy* by Dianna Hutts Aston
- *My Favorite Tree* by Diane Iverson
- (optional) *Crinkleroot's Guide to Knowing the Trees* by Jim Arnosky (out of print)
- *The Robins in Your Backyard* by Nancy Carol Willis
- *From Seed To Plant* by Gail Gibbons
- *Bumblebee at Apple Tree Lane* by Laura Gates Galvin
- (optional) *The Owl and the Woodpecker: Encounters with North America's Most Iconic Birds* by Paul Bannick
- *Are You a Dragonfly?* By Judy Allen and Tudor Humphries
- *Flower Garden* by Eve Bunting
- (optional) *Wonderful Pussy Willows* by Jerome Wexler (out of print)
- *Flip, Float, Fly!: Seeds on the Move* by JoAnn Early Macken
- *Water Dance* by Thomas Locker
- *Wasps* by Martha Rustad
- *Chippy Chipmunk Parties in the Garden* by Kathy M. Miller
- (optional) *Read-Aloud Poems for Young People* OR *The Oxford Book of Children's Verse in America*

For nature studies

- Variety of apples; knife
- Shovel; large glass jar; smaller jar or container; dirt; dead leaves
- Several potted flowers of the same kind; gauze/netting (optional)
- (optional) Suet
- Variety of flower seeds in packets; containers; soil

Lesson 1

Checklist

• *Outdoor Secrets*

Read together the chapter "How the Apple Blossom Came Back" in *Outdoor Secrets*. Ask for an oral narration.

Lesson 2

Checklist

• *Favorite Poems Old and New*
• Apple; knife
• Nature notebook

Ask your child what he remembers from last time's reading about the apple blossom. Read together "A Comparison" by John Farrar in *Favorite Poems Old and New*, page 214.

Cut open an apple from side to side, not top to bottom, in order to see the blossom imprint. Have your child draw in his nature notebook the apple half with its blossom imprint.

Lesson 3

Checklist

• *How Do Apples Grow*
• Nature notebook

Read together *How Do Apples Grow* by Betsy Maestro. Add any interesting information to your child's nature notebook's apple page.

Lesson 4

Checklist

• A variety of apples
• Chart on page 13

Get three or four different kinds of apples from the grocery store; for

Tip: You can learn more about apples and apple trees in The Handbook of Nature Study, *pages 661–670, lessons 182, 183, and 184.*

Reminder: Get How Do Apples Grow *by Betsy Maestro for lesson 3 and* Johnny Appleseed *by Reeve Lindbergh for lesson 5.*

Tip: You don't have to buy a whole bag of each kind of apple. Just buy one of each if you want to.

Notes

Tip: If possible, arrange to visit an orchard to see live apple trees.

Reminder: Get *A Desert Scrapbook: Dawn to Dusk in the Sonoran Desert by Virginia Wright-Frierson for lesson 8.*

example, Granny Smith, Red Delicious, Braeburn, Gala. First, have your child look at the apples and describe each one's shape. Record his observations on the chart on page 13. Second, have him compare the apples' colors, and record those observations on the chart. Then let him taste each apple and compare their flavors; record those observations too.

Lesson 5

Checklist

• *Johnny Appleseed*
• Nature notebook

Read together the poem in book form, *Johnny Appleseed* by Reeve Lindbergh. If your child has a favorite line or two from the poem, have him copy those words into his nature notebook.

Lesson 6

Checklist

• *Outdoor Secrets*

Read together the chapter "The Century-Plant's Wish" from *Outdoor Secrets*. Ask for an oral narration.

Lesson 7

Checklist

• Picture of a Century plant
• Nature notebook

Tip: You will find some links to pictures and information on a Century plant on the Links & Tips page for this book on our Web site: simplycharlottemason.com/books/outdoor-secrets/links-tips

Ask your child what he remembers from last time's reading about the Century plant. Explain that a Century plant belongs to the same family as a cactus. Show your child a picture of the plant in a book or on the Internet. If you have an aloe plant in your home, you could compare it to that.

Read together the two quotes on page 14 and discuss what they mean. Add one or both to your child's nature notebook, if desired.

What I Noticed About These Apples

Kind of Apple	Shape	Color	Flavor

Notes

Tip: *If you have a botanical garden nearby that has a desert room, arrange to visit it.*

Reminder: *Get* An Earthworm's Life *by John Himmelman for lesson 11.*

Tip: *You can find out more about earthworms in* The Handbook of Nature Study, *pages 422–425, lesson 107.*

"We could never learn to be brave and patient, if there were only joy in the world."—Helen Keller

"How poor are they who have not patience! What wound did ever heal but by degrees."—Shakespeare

Lesson 8

Checklist

• *A Desert Scrapbook: Dawn to Dusk in the Sonoran Desert*

Read together about other cactus plants and life in the desert in *A Desert Scrapbook: Dawn to Dusk in the Sonoran Desert.*

Lesson 9

Checklist

• *Outdoor Secrets*

Read together the chapter "The Uninvited Guest" from *Outdoor Secrets.* Ask for an oral narration.

Lesson 10

Checklist

• (optional) Shovel
• (optional) Large glass jar; smaller jar; dirt; dead leaves
• Nature notebook

Ask your child what he remembers from last time's reading about the earthworm. Do one or more of the nature study ideas below.
• Dig for worms and observe their movements.
• Examine an earthworm closely; look at the rings on its body; carefully pull it through your fingers to feel its bristles. Have your child draw an earthworm in his nature notebook.
• Create an earthworm "farm." Get a large glass jar and put a smaller jar or other smaller container inside it. Fill the space between the jars with dirt. Moisten the dirt and place several earthworms in it. Place a layer of dead

leaves on top for the earthworms to eat. Put the jar in a cool, dark place and observe it over several days. You should be able to see how the worms make tunnels in the dirt. If desired, have your child draw a picture of the tunnels in his nature notebook. Don't forget to release the worms when you are finished observing them.

Lesson 11

Checklist

• *An Earthworm's Life*
• Nature notebook

Read together *An Earthworm's Life* by John Himmelman. Add any interesting facts about worms to your nature notebook.

Lesson 12

Checklist

• *Outdoor Secrets*

Read together the chapter "What the Golden-Rod Did" from *Outdoor Secrets*. Ask for an oral narration.

Lesson 13

Checklist

• *Favorite Poems Old and New*
• Picture of goldenrod
• Nature notebook

Ask your child what he remembers from last time's reading about goldenrod. Show your child a picture of the plant in a book or on the Internet.

Read together one or more of the poems below and on page 16. If your child has a favorite line or two from one of the poems, have him copy those words into his nature notebook.

Poems

"The Golden Rod" by Frank Dempster Sherman in *Favorite Poems Old and New*, page 221

Notes

Reminder: Get A Seed Is Sleepy *by Dianna Hutts Aston for lesson 14.*

Tip: You can learn more about goldenrod in The Handbook of Nature Study, *pages 503–506, lesson 132.*

Tip: You will find some links to pictures and information on goldenrod on the Links & Tips page for this book on our Web site: simplycharlottemason. com/books/outdoor-secrets/ links-tips

Notes

September
by Helen Hunt Jackson

The goldenrod is yellow;
The corn is turning brown;
The trees in apple orchards
With fruit are bending down.

The gentian's bluest fringes
Are curling in the sun;
In dusty pods the milkweed
Its hidden silk has spun.

The sedges flaunt their harvest
In every meadow nook;
And asters by the brook-side
Make asters in the brook.

From dewy lanes at morning
The grapes' sweet odors rise;
At noon the roads all flutter
With yellow butterflies.

By all these lovely tokens
September days are here,
With summer's best of weather,
And autumn's best of cheer.

I am alone with nature
by Mary Clemmer Ames

I am alone with nature,
With the soft September day;
The lifting hills above me,
With goldenrod are gay.
Across the fields of ether
Flit butterflies at play;
And cones of garnet sumac
Glow down the country way.

The autumn dandelion
Beside the roadway burns;
Above the lichened boulders
Quiver the pluméd ferns.
The cream-white silk of the milkweed
Floats from its sea-green pod;
From out the mossy rock-seams
Flashes the goldenrod.

Lesson 14

Checklist

• *A Seed Is Sleepy*

Read together *A Seed Is Sleepy* by Dianna Hutts Aston.

Lesson 15

Checklist

• *Outdoor Secrets*

Read together the chapter "The Horse Chestnut's Name" from *Outdoor Secrets*. Ask for an oral narration.

Lesson 16

Checklist

• Nature notebook

Do one or more of the nature study ideas below.
• Find as many as you can of the trees mentioned in the story of the Horse Chestnut's Name. Have your child draw the basic shapes of the trees in his nature notebook.
• Pick a leaf from each tree and either draw them, do a leaf rubbing of them, or press them. Label each one and you'll create your own field guide of trees in your neighborhood.
• Have your child draw the seeds of the trees or glue them in his nature notebook if they are flat.

Lesson 17

Checklist

• *My Favorite Tree*
• (optional) *Crinkleroot's Guide to Knowing the Trees*

Read together *My Favorite Tree* by Diane Iverson.
If you can find a copy of *Crinkleroot's Guide to Knowing the Trees* by Jim Arnosky, read it together too. This great book is out of print, but it may be available at your local library.

Notes

Tip: The term "naked" seed is an accurate scientific term.

Reminder: Get My Favorite Tree *by Diane Iverson for lesson 17. If available, also get* Crinkleroot's Guide to Knowing Trees *by Jim Arnosky.*

Tip: You can learn more about the Horse Chestnut tree in The Handbook of Nature Study, *pages 648–650, lesson 178.*

Tip: To do a leaf rubbing, put a sheet of drawing paper on top of the leaf. Make sure the leaf is top-side-down; you will get more detail from the back of the leaf. Unwrap the paper wrapper from a crayon and rub the crayon on the paper over the leaf. Be sure to rub with the side of the crayon, rather than with the point.

Tip: To press a leaf, enclose the leaf between sheets of paper towel or waxed paper and slip it into the middle pages of a large, heavy book. Check your leaves after a few days and see how flat they are.

Lesson 18

Checklist

• Nature notebook

Read aloud one or more of the poems below. If your child has a favorite line or two from one of the poems, have him copy those words into his nature notebook.

Poems

Tree Feelings
by Charlotte Perkins Stetson

I wonder if they like it—being trees?
I suppose they do.
It must feel so good to have the ground so flat,
And feel yourself stand straight up like that.
So stiff in the middle, and then branch at ease,
Big boughs that arch, small ones that bend and blow,
And all those fringy leaves that flutter so.
You'd think they'd break off at the lower end
When the wind fills them, and their great heads bend.
But when you think of all the roots they drop,
As much at bottom as there is on top,
A double tree, widespread in earth and air,
Like a reflection in the water there.

Trees
by Joyce Kilmer

I think that I shall never see
A poem lovely as a tree.

A tree whose hungry mouth is pressed
Against the earth's sweet flowing breast;

A tree that looks at God all day
And lifts her leafy arms to pray;

A tree that may in summer wear
A nest of robins in her hair;

Upon whose bosom snow has lain;
Who intimately lives with rain.

Poems are made by fools like me,
But only God can make a tree.

Trees
by Sara Coleridge

The oak is called the king of trees,
The aspen quivers in the breeze,
The poplar grows up straight and tall,
The peach tree spreads along the wall,
The sycamore gives pleasant shade,
The willow droops in watery glade,
The fir tree useful timber gives,
The beech amid the forest lives.

Lesson 19

Checklist

• *Outdoor Secrets*

While you're learning about trees, go ahead and read together the chapter "The Disobedient Tree" from *Outdoor Secrets*. Ask for an oral narration.

Lesson 20

Checklist

• *Favorite Poems Old and New*
• Nature notebook

Ask your child what he remembers from last time's reading about the cherry tree. Read aloud the poem "Oh, Fair to See" by Christina Rossetti from *Favorite Poems Old and New*, page 215. If your child has a favorite line or two from the poem, have him copy those words into his nature notebook.

Lesson 21

Checklist

• Outdoor Secrets

Read together the chapter "A Rainy Day Sermon" from *Outdoor Secrets*. Ask for an oral narration.

Reminder: Get The Robins in Your Backyard *by Nancy Carol Willis for lesson 22.*

Notes

Tip: You can learn more about robins in The Handbook of Nature Study, *pages 57–62, lesson 11.*

Lesson 22

Checklist

- *The Robins in Your Backyard*
- Nature notebook

Read together *The Robins in Your Backyard* by Nancy Carol Willis.

Look for robins outside to observe and have your child draw them in his nature notebook. If you cannot find a live robin to study, draw a picture based on one in *The Robins in Your Backyard*. If it is spring or early summer, look for robins' nests and observe the parents' actions too. Record your child's observations in his nature notebook.

Lesson 23

Checklist

- *Outdoor Secrets*

While you are learning about robins, go ahead and read together the chapter "Two True Stories about Robins" from *Outdoor Secrets*. Ask for an oral narration.

Lesson 24

Checklist

- *Favorite Poems Old and New*
- Nature notebook

Read aloud one or more of the poems below and on page 21. If your child has a favorite line or two from one of the poems, have him copy those words into his nature notebook.

Poems

"What Robin Told" by George Cooper from *Favorite Poems Old and New*, page 285

Reminder: Get From Seed To Plant *by Gail Gibbons for lesson 27 and* Bumblebee at Apple Tree Lane *by Laura Gates Galvin for lesson 28.*

A Bird Came Down
by Emily Dickinson

A bird came down the walk:
He did not know I saw;
He bit an angle-worm in halves
And ate the fellow, raw.

*And then he drank a dew
From a convenient grass,
And then hopped sidewise to the wall
To let a beetle pass.*

*He glanced with rapid eyes
That hurried all abroad,—
They looked like frightened beads, I thought
He stirred his velvet head*

*Like one in danger; cautious,
I offered him a crumb,
And he unrolled his feathers
And rowed him softer home*

*Than oars divide the ocean,
Too silver for a seam,
Or butterflies, off banks of noon,
Leap, plashless, as they swim.*

The Robin
by Emily Dickinson

*The robin is the one
That interrupts the morn
With hurried, few, express reports
When March is scarcely on.*

*The robin is the one
That overflows the noon
With her cherubic quantity,
As April has begun.*

*The robin is the one
That speechless from her nest
Submits that home and certainty
And sanctity are best.*

Lesson 25

Checklist

• *Outdoor Secrets*

Read together the chapter "The Selfish Salvia" from *Outdoor Secrets*. Ask for an oral narration.

Tip: You can learn more about salvia in The Handbook of Nature Study, *pages 579–581, lesson 161.*

Notes

Lesson 26

Checklist

- Potted flowers
- Gauze or netting (optional)
- Nature notebook

Tip: You can get a flat of flowers pretty inexpensively at a local gardening center in the spring or summer.

Ask your child what he remembers from last time's reading about the selfish salvia. Learn more about pollinating by doing one or more of these nature study ideas.

- Choose several potted flowers of the same kind. Keep some flowers inside or leave them outside but cover them with gauze/netting to prevent insects from pollinating them. Let the other flowers grow as normal. Observe how the plants grow over time and what differences there are in growth between the protected plants and the "normal" plants. Record your observations in your child's nature notebook.
- Go outside and observe bees and other insects pollinating flowers. Have your child draw what he sees in his nature notebook.

If available, get The Owl and the Woodpecker: Encounters with North America's Most Iconic Birds *by Paul Bannick for lesson 30.*

Lesson 27

Checklist

- *From Seed to Plant*
- *Favorite Poems Old and New*
- Nature notebook

Read together *From Seed to Plant* by Gail Gibbons. Help your child draw in his nature notebook the process of seeds growing into flowers.

Read aloud the poem "Flowers" by Harry Behn in *Favorite Poems Old and New*, page 222.

Lesson 28

Checklist

- *Bumblebee at Apple Tree Lane*
- *Favorite Poems Old and New*
- Nature notebook

Tip: You can learn more about bumblebees in The Handbook of Nature Study, *pages 389–391, lesson 98.*

Read together *Bumblebee at Apple Tree Lane* by Laura Gates Galvin.

Also read aloud the poem "How Doth the Little Busy Bee" by Isaac Watts in *Favorite Poems Old and New*, page 125. Copy the poem into your child's nature notebook, if desired.

Lesson 29

Checklist

• *Outdoor Secrets*

Read together the chapter "Who Knocked?" from *Outdoor Secrets*. Ask for an oral narration.

Tip: *You can learn more about flickers in* The Handbook of Nature Study, *pages 77–80, lesson 18.*

Lesson 30

Checklist

• (optional) *The Owl and the Woodpecker*
• (optional) Suet
• Nature notebook

Learn more about flickers, and woodpeckers in general, by doing one or more of these nature study ideas.

• Use *The Owl and the Woodpecker: Encounters with North America's Most Iconic Birds* by Paul Bannick as a picture reference book. (Don't worry about reading the text. Just enjoy the beautiful pictures.) You child could draw several different types of woodpeckers in different poses in his nature notebook. Be sure to label them.

• Put suet out for the birds, then identify and draw the woodpeckers that come to eat it.

Reminder: *Get* Are You a Dragonfly? *By Judy Allen and Tudor Humphries for lesson 33.*

Lesson 31

Checklist

• *Outdoor Secrets*

Read together the chapter "The Bumblebee's Mistake" from *Outdoor Secrets*. Ask for an oral narration.

Tip: *You can learn more about dragonflies in* The Handbook of Nature Study, *pages 401–408, lesson 103.*

Lesson 32

Checklist

• *Favorite Poems Old and New*
• Nature notebook

Notes

Reminder: Get Flower Garden *by Eve Bunting for lesson 36 and* Flip, Float, Fly!: Seeds on the Move *by JoAnn Early Macken for lesson 38. If available, get* Wonderful Pussy Willows *by Jerome Wexler for lesson 37.*

Tip: One of the statements in the "Did You Know" section in the back of Are You a Dragonfly? *reports that dragonflies have been around for "300 million years." Use that statement to discuss evolution, or skip that statement entirely.*

Tip: You can learn more about studying plants in The Handbook of Nature Study, *pages 453–456.*

Read aloud the poem "A Dragon-Fly" by Eleanor Farjeon in *Favorite Poems Old and New,* page 130. If your child has a favorite line or two from the poem, have him copy those words into his nature notebook.

Lesson 33

Checklist

• *Are You a Dragonfly?*

Read together *Are You a Dragonfly?* by Judy Allen and Tudor Humphries.

Lesson 34

Checklist

• *Outdoor Secrets*

Read together the chapter "A Brave Plant" from *Outdoor Secrets.* Ask for an oral narration.

Lesson 35

Checklist

• Flower seeds; containers; soil
• Nature notebook

Learn more about flowers by growing some of your own from seeds. Here's how. Be sure to record the entire process in your nature notebook.

1. Get a variety of flower seeds in packets.
2. Soak the flower seeds overnight.
3. Follow the seed packets' directions to plant them. Be sure to label the containers.
4. Water your containers often and keep them in a sunny spot. You want to keep the soil moist.
5. When your seeds have grown into seedlings, transplant them into bigger pots, a window box, or a garden outdoors.

Lesson 36

Checklist

- *Flower Garden*
- *Favorite Poems Old and New*
- Nature notebook

Read together *Flower Garden* by Eve Bunting. Spend time pointing out the different kinds of flowers in the window box when you get to that page. After you've finished the book, go back and see how many of the flowers your child can remember the names of.

Read aloud "Window Boxes" by Eleanor Farjeon in *Favorite Poems Old and New*, page 222.

Have your child draw at least three kinds of flowers in his nature notebook and label them. He can draw them from the illustration in *Flower Garden* or take a field trip to see some real flowers at a local nursery, garden, or front porch.

Lesson 37

Checklist

- *Outdoor Secrets*
- (optional) *Wonderful Pussy Willows*

Read together the chapter "The Sower" from *Outdoor Secrets*. Ask for an oral narration.

Also, if you can find a copy, *Wonderful Pussy Willows* by Jerome Wexler is a great book to read. It is out of print, but your local library may have it.

Tip: You can learn more about pussy willows in The Handbook of Nature Study, *pages 651–655, lesson 179.*

Lesson 38

Checklist

- *Flip, Float, Fly!*

Ask your child what he remembers from last time's reading about the "sower." Read together *Flip, Float, Fly!: Seeds on the Move* by JoAnn Early Macken.

Lesson 39

Checklist

- Nature notebook

Reminder: *Get* Water Dance *by Thomas Locker for lesson 42 and* Wasps *by Martha Rustad for lesson 44.*

Notes

Learn more about seed dispersion by gathering as many different seeds as you can find outdoors. Examine them to see if you can determine which method of spreading each seed would use. For example, a dandelion's or milkweed's seeds are light and fluffy and would disperse in the wind. An acorn is heavy and would fall to the ground. A sweetgum seed is prickly and would stick to a passing animal or sock and be carried to another section of ground. Record your observations in your child's nature notebook; draw the seeds and label how they spread.

Lesson 40

Checklist

• *Outdoor Secrets*

Read together the chapter "The Baby Plants' Bed Coverings" from *Outdoor Secrets*. Ask for an oral narration.

Lesson 41

Checklist

• *Favorite Poems Old and New*
• Nature notebook

Ask your child what he remembers from last time's reading about the baby plants. Read aloud the poem "Baby Seed Song" by E. Nesbit in *Favorite Poems Old and New*, page 215.

If it is fall, go outside and collect a variety of leaves. Compare their colors and have your child draw them in his nature notebook.

Lesson 42

Checklist

• *Water Dance*
• *Favorite Poems Old and New*
• Nature notebook

Tip: *You can learn more about the forms of water in* The Handbook of Nature Study, *pages 808–814, lesson 223.*

Learn more about the role water plays in its various forms by reading *Water Dance* by Thomas Locker.

Go outside with a blanket, lie down and spend some time looking at the clouds. Have your child draw some in his nature notebook.

Read aloud the poem "The Cloud" by Percy Bysshe Shelley in *Favorite Poems Old and New*, page 76.

Lesson 43

Checklist

• *Outdoor Secrets*

Read together the chapter "A Family Quarrel" from *Outdoor Secrets*. Ask for an oral narration.

Lesson 44

Checklist

• *Wasps*
• Nature notebook

Ask your child what he remembers from last time's reading about wasps. Read together *Wasps* by Martha Rustad. Record any interesting facts in your child's nature notebook.

Lesson 45

Checklist

• *Outdoor Secrets*

Read together the chapter "The Idle Chipmunk" from *Outdoor Secrets*. Ask for an oral narration.

Lesson 46

Checklist

• *Chippy Chipmunk Parties in the Garden*

Notes

Reminder: Get Chippy Chipmunk Parties in the Garden *by Kathy M. Miller for lesson 46. If readily available, get* Read-Aloud Poems for Young People *or* The Oxford Book of Children's Verse in America *for lesson 47.*

Tip: You can learn more about chipmunks in The Handbook of Nature Study, *pages 239–241, lesson 58.*

Notes

Ask your child what he remembers from last time's reading about the chipmunk. Read together *Chippy Chipmunk Parties in the Garden* by Kathy M. Miller.

Lesson 47

Checklist

- *Chippy Chipmunk Parties in the Garden*
- Nature notebook
- (optional) *Read-Aloud Poems for Young People* or *The Oxford Book of Children's Verse in America*

Have your child draw in his nature notebook a favorite chipmunk pose from the book, *Chippy Chipmunk Parties in the Garden.*

If you happen to have a copy of *Read-Aloud Poems for Young People* or *The Oxford Book of Children's Verse in America,* read aloud the poem "The Chipmunk's Day" by Randall Jarrell. If your child has a favorite line or two from the poem, have him copy those words into his nature notebook.

Lesson 48

Checklist

- *Outdoor Secrets*

Read together the chapter "The Troubled Apple-Tree" from *Outdoor Secrets*. Ask for an oral narration.

Lesson 49

Checklist

- Nature notebook

Ask your child what he remembers from last time's reading about the troubled apple tree.

Read aloud "The Planting of the Apple Tree" by William Cullen Bryant (on the next page). If your child has a favorite line or two from the poem, have him copy those words into his nature notebook.

The Planting of the Apple Tree
by William Cullen Bryant

What plant we in this apple tree?
Buds, which the breath of summer days
Shall lengthen into leafy sprays;
Boughs where the thrush, with crimson breast,
Shall haunt and sing and hide her nest;
We plant, upon the sunny lea,
A shadow for the noontide hour;
A shelter from the summer shower,
When we plant the apple tree.

What plant we in this apple tree?
Fruits that shall swell in sunny June,
And redden in the August noon,
And drop, when gentle airs come by,
That fan the blue September sky,
While children come, with cries of glee,
And seek them where the fragrant grass
Betrays their bed to those who pass,
At the foot of the apple tree.

Lesson 50

Notes

Checklist

• Nature notebook

Discuss how the troubled apple tree missed the importance of the bird rubbing its beak on the branch. Why might the troubled apple tree not have noticed what the bird was really doing? Talk about what we might miss if we are not paying close attention and patiently observing what is going on around us in nature.

Go outside and practice using different senses to observe quietly and patiently. Challenge your child to sit perfectly quiet with his eyes closed for three minutes (if he can), then tell you everything he heard. Record his observations in his nature notebook. Have him sit perfectly still and watch a particular animal or insect closely for three minutes (or however long is appropriate for your child). Record his observations in his nature notebook.

Encourage your child to continue discovering outdoor secrets that are all around him.

Tip: Charlotte Mason said, "Children should be encouraged to watch, patiently and quietly, until they learn something of the habits and history of bee, ant, wasp, spider, hairy caterpillar, dragon-fly, and whatever of larger growth comes in their way. 'The creatures never have any habits while I am looking!' a little girl in some story-book is made to complain: but that was her fault; the bright keen eyes with which children are blest were made to see, and see into, the doings of creatures too small for the unaided observation of older people" (Vol. 1, p. 57).